Selections from the

Rime Spirituali

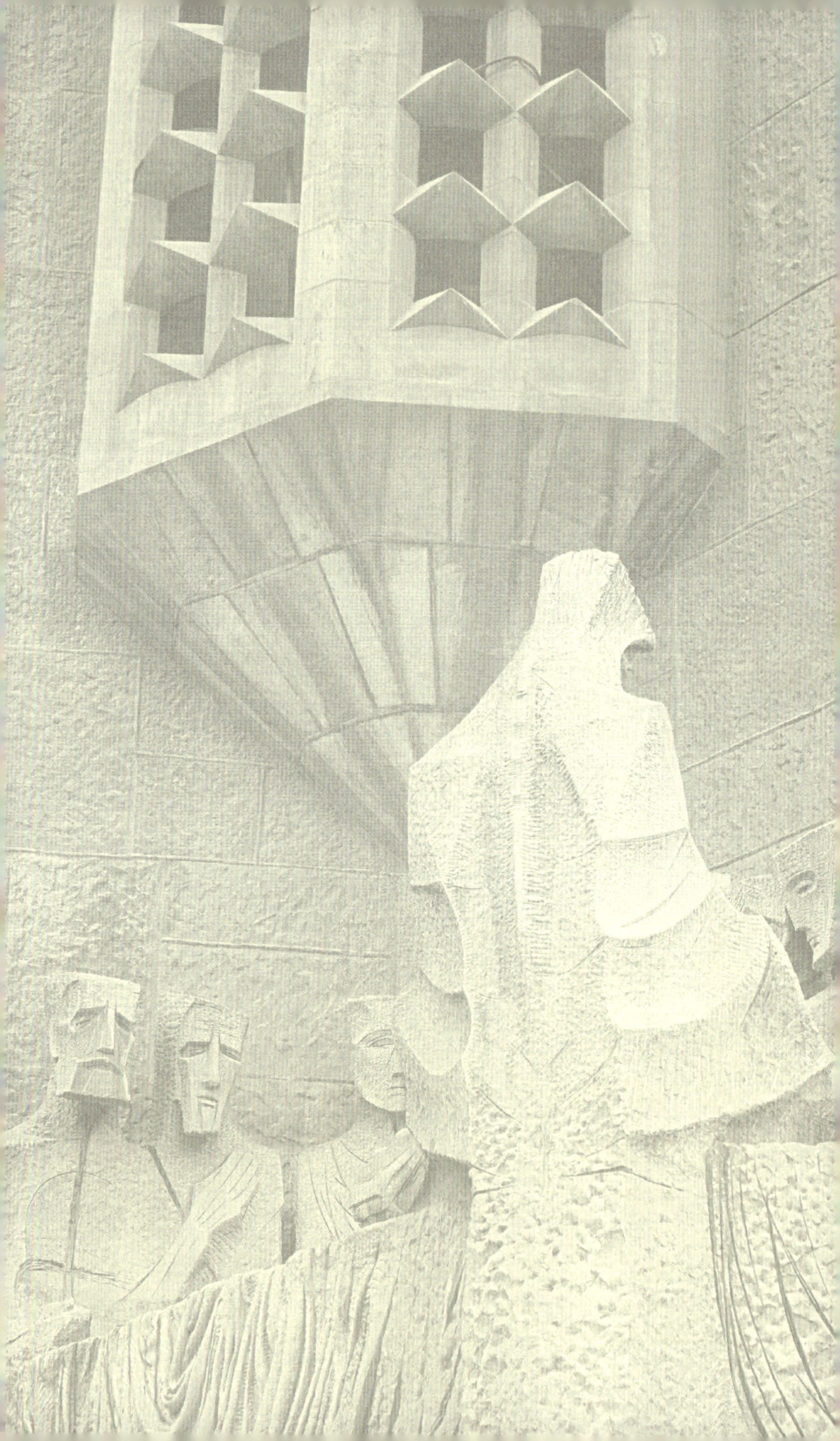

English Texts by Jan Zwicky

VITTORIA COLONNA

Selections from the Rime Spirituali

with photographs of

Josep Maria Subirachs' Passion Façade

PHOTOGRAPHS BY

ROBERT MOODY

The Porcupine's Quill

Library and Archives Canada Cataloguing in Publication

Colonna, Vittoria, 1492–1547, author
Vittoria Colonna : selections from the Rime spirituali with photographs of Josep Maria Subirachs' Passion Façade / English texts by Jan Zwicky ; photographs by Robert Moody.

This volume reproduces ten of Vittoria Colonna's sonnets with English versions based on the English translations originally published in *Sonnets for Michelangelo*, c2005. Text in Italian with English text on facing pages.

ISBN: 978-0-88984-370-7 (pbk.)

1. Colonna, Vittoria, 1492–1547—Translations into English. 2. Sonnets, Italian—Translations into English. 3. Christian poetry, Italian—Translations into English. 4. Subirachs, José Maria, 1927– Passion Façade. I. Zwicky, Jan, 1955–, translator II. Moody, Robert, 1941–, illustrator III. Title.

PQ4620.A2 2014 851'.3 C2014-900883-X

1 2 3 4 • 16 15 14

Published by The Porcupine's Quill, P.O. Box 160, Erin, Ontario NOB 1TO. http://porcupinesquill.ca

Represented in Canada by Canadian Manda. Trade orders are available from University of Toronto Press. We acknowledge the support of the Ontario Arts Council and the Canada Council for the Arts for our publishing program. The financial support of the Government of Canada through the Book Publishing Industry Development Program is also gratefully acknowledged.

Canada Council for the Arts / Conseil des Arts du Canada

Canada

ONTARIO ARTS COUNCIL
CONSEIL DES ARTS DE L'ONTARIO
an Ontario government agency
un organisme du gouvernement de l'Ontario

Ontario
Ontario Media Development Corporation

dedicated to the loving memory
of Marian Moody,

wife of RM
and friend of us both

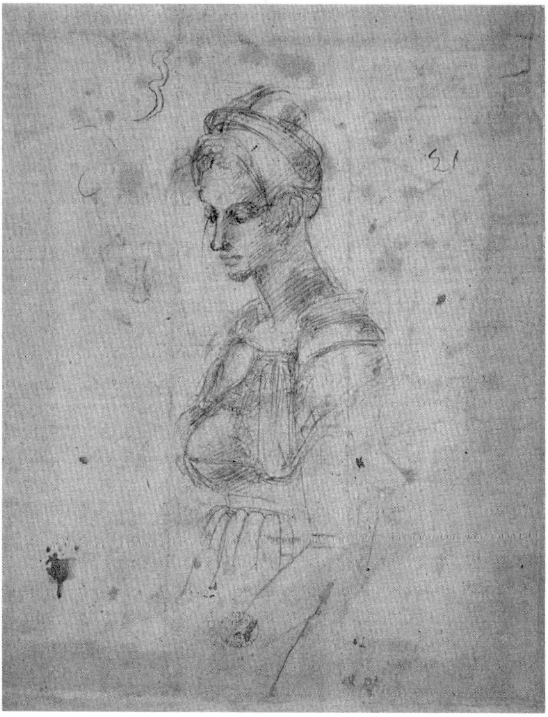

Figure of a woman seated slightly, c. 1525 Michelangelo.
Courtesy of the British Museum.

Vittoria Colonna was born into a rich and powerful family at Marino, near Rome, in 1490 or 1492. She was betrothed at a very young age to Francesco Ferrante D'Avalos, and in 1509 was married to him. They lived together near Naples for two years before D'Avalos left to fight in the wars against the French. She saw him only infrequently after that, although they corresponded. There were no children, and in 1525 D'Avalos died as a result of injuries sustained at the battle of Pavia.

Colonna retreated to the convent of San Silvestro in Rome and professed a desire to take orders but was forbidden to do so by both her brother and the pope. It is thought that, although they belonged to opposing factions, both men were alert to her political value as a marriageable property and did not want her sequestered in a convent. Colonna did not, however, remarry, and this refusal appears to have been crucial to her success as a writer.

She made her reputation as a *univira*—a once-married woman who remains loyal to her dead husband. By this means, whether innocently or with forethought, she was able to defuse the intense hostility usually displayed towards women who attempted to cultivate a public voice. Such women, unless they were nuns of spotless repute, were routinely denounced as lascivious whores—insufficiently under the thumb of their male relatives, and so likely to subvert the lines of patriarchal inheritance. But the adoring married love Colonna celebrates in her early poems, the so-called *rime amorose*, was regarded with approbation by the male establishment, despite its secular nature. And so she became a model for other women poets of the period: they were subsequently able to find their way into print citing Colonna as their exemplar.

At first Colonna's work circulated privately, but as her reputation grew, so did the interest of publishers. In 1535, ten years after D'Avalos's death and at the end of her self-imposed period of mourning, Colonna allowed a sonnet she had composed for Pietro Bembo to be published in the second edition of his own *Rime*, which Bembo brought out in 1535. In 1538, *Rime de la Divina Vittoria Colonna Marchesa di Pescara* was published, without Colonna's authorization, in Parma by Philippo Pirogallo. Thirteen subsequent editions followed during her lifetime, and nine after her death. The first four of these contained only selections from the *rime amorose*, but all subsequent editions, starting in 1539, included examples of her so-called *rime spirituali*, the meditative religious poems to which she turned in the later part of her life.

In the late 1530s, Colonna returned to San Silvestro. An intense friendship with Michelangelo began in this period, and she compiled a gift manuscript for him around 1540, consisting of 103 *rime spirituali*. The manuscript is plainly bound and there is evidence that Colonna closely supervised its preparation. In many instances, versions of the poems that appear in the manuscript are materially different from versions that appeared in print. About the same time, Michelangelo gave her a series of three presentation drawings exploring Christian themes that figure centrally in Colonna's work. The two are said to have talked long hours together, and they wrote to one another frequently. Michelangelo's sonnets and madrigals to Colonna are among the finest and most passionate he wrote: it appears that she was the last, and perhaps greatest, love of his life. Colonna's sonnets are more oblique in their address; it is always possible to read them as purely religious meditations. Nonetheless, if we imagine them written for and presented to Michelangelo, there can be little doubt of her deep and intimate regard.

Colonna was interested in religious reform, and from the late 1520s was repeatedly drawn into association, and in some cases close friendships, with reformers. The presence of reformist ideas is marked in the sonnets, particularly the idea that genuine faith rather than institutional observance is essential for salvation. Colonna does not write, however, as someone attempting to paraphrase ideas not entirely her own. She writes with the directness and intensity that attend personal vision. Indeed, central images and core vocabulary are carried over from the *rime amorose* into the *rime spirituali* to striking effect. Her work is—to use a word that figures frequently in her own poetry—ardent. And it was this, I believe, that drew Michelangelo most strongly to her. He found in Colonna someone who understood life as he did: a passionate endeavour to come to grips with spiritual truth.

Colonna died in poor health in the Convent of Sant'Anna de' Funari in 1547. Michelangelo was distraught at her death and following it retreated from society for the remainder of his own life.

⋆

The English poems that appear here do not reproduce Colonna's originals word for word or even phrase for phrase: they are what I call versions rather than translations. In a scholarly context it would be right, indeed essential, to try to give readers a sense of her immense skill as a writer of Renaissance Italian verse. But in a literary context, an attempt to reproduce her Petrarchan rhetoric and logic, would, I believe, amount to a kind of misrepresentation—a failure to draw a distinction between her rich and antique clothing and her equally remarkable character. No doubt the two are related, and sometimes intricately so. But Colonna believed, as do I, that it is possible to experience character independently of costume. It is that character I have attempted to convey here.

I have relied heavily on Abigail Brundin's fine *en face* edition of the sonnets, *Sonnets for Michelangelo: A Bilingual Edition* (University of Chicago Press, 2005). It is her edition of the Italian, based on the texts in the Codice Vaticano Latino 11539, that I have followed here. I strongly recommend both her annotated translations and her introductory essay to all readers interested in exploring Colonna's work further.

⋆

I was led to Colonna's work by accident, in the course of attempting to confirm something about Michelangelo's, and I was inspired to follow up out of purely intellectual and artistic curiosity. That is, I am not and have never been a professing Christian. My interest in Colonna's spiritual beliefs is real, but ecumenical. My admiration for her intelligence and courage remains boundless.

JZ, *Heriot Ridge, July 2012*

The photographs that interleave the poems of Vittoria Colonna in this volume are not intended to speak directly to her thought but rather to form a backdrop or canvas for the deeply Christian sentiments on which they are based. With the exception of one, they are photographs of Josep Maria Subirachs' Passion Façade, which is part of the exterior of the basilica of the Sagrada Familia in Barcelona. In the sparse, lean, angular figures and the strong geometry of the settings, the story of the suffering and tragedy of the passion of Christ loses none of its universal power. In fact quite the opposite. As with Jan Zwicky's versions of Colonna's poems, the modern aesthetic brings new freshness and insight to these classical themes.

The Passion Façade was part of Antonio Gaudi's personal vision for the basilica and arose from his own experience of intense suffering, though the actual design of the sculptures was never completed in his lifetime. When Subirachs was commissioned to create the work, his single request was that he be free to follow his own artistic muse. The resulting work is something very different from anything Gaudi would have envisioned. As Subirachs points out, Gaudi believed that the curve, with its rounded and organic fluidity, was the true line of God. Subirachs' geometry is starkly linear and angular, but speaks well to the dramatic tensions of the passion story.

The single exception to the work of Subirachs among these photographs is the view upwards into the light-filled central spire of the basilica (p. 53). This is pure Gaudi. We offer it as a visual correspondence to the final transcendence described in the Christian story.

RM, *Victoria, July 2012*

Selections from the Rime Spirituali

1

Poi che 'l mio casto amor gran tempo tenne
l'alma di fama accesa, ed ella un angue
in sen nudriò per cui dolente or langue
volta al Signor, onde 'l rimedio venne,
i santi chiodi omai sian le mie penne,
e puro inchiostro il prezioso sangue,
vergata carta il sacro corpo exangue,
sì ch'io scriva ad altrui quel ch'ei sostenne.
Chiamar qui non convien Parnaso o Delo,
ch'ad altra aqua s'aspira, ad altro monte
si poggia, u' piede uman per sé non sale.
Quel sol, che alluma gli elementi e 'l cielo,
prego ch'aprendo il suo lucido fonte
mi porga umor a la gran sete eguale.

1

All the while my widowed love
flushed me with thoughts of literary fame,
it fed a serpent in my breast
and now, afflicted, languishing,
my only remedy is God.
                                        From now on,
let the sweet nails be my quills,
his blood my ink, my text
his scored and sacred body.
No more Parnassus, no more Delos:
I must labour over other mountains,
other seas.
                    And pray to the sun,
which lights up earth and sky,
that he will loose his shining spring,
pour me water equal to my thirst.

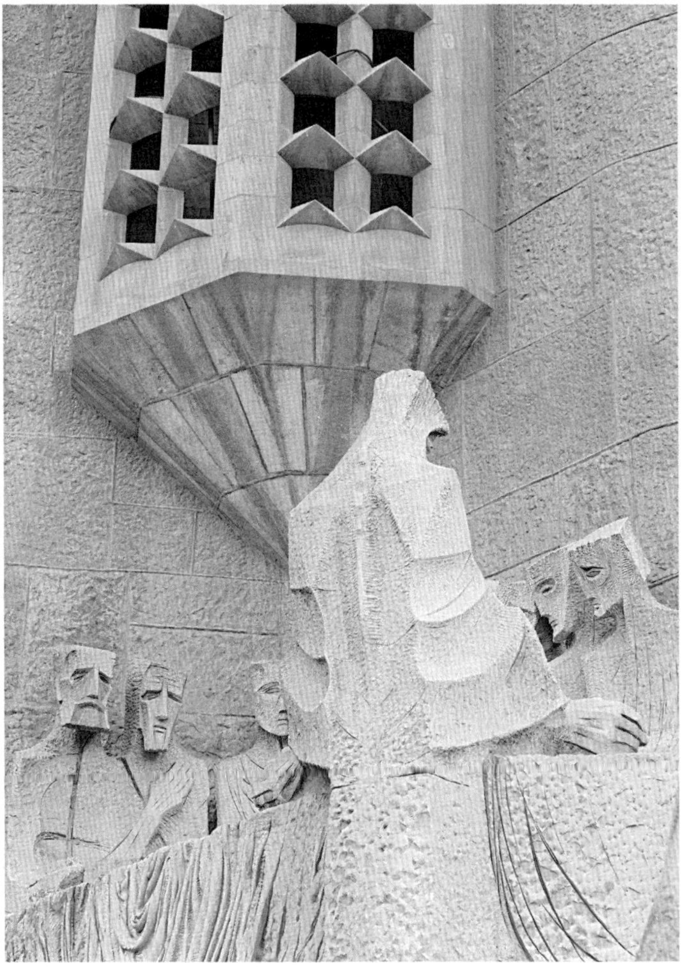

21

Debile e 'nferma a la salute vera
ricorro, e cieca il sol cui solo adoro
invoco, e nuda bramo il celest'oro
e vo al suo foco fredda in pura cera;
e quanto in sé disfida, tanto spera
l'alma in quel d'ogni ben vivo tesoro,
che la può far con largo ampio ristoro
sana, ricca, al suo caldo arder sincera.
Onde con questi doni e questo ardire
lo veggia non col mio ma col suo lume,
l'ami e ringratii col suo stesso amore.
Non saranno alor mie l'opre e 'l desire,
ma lieve andrò con le celesti piume
ove mi spinge e tira il santo ardore.

21

Weak and sick, I run again
toward salvation: I call out
to the sun, the one thing I adore.
Naked, cold as wax,
but greedy for his golden fire,
I go. Equal to my illness is my hope
for his huge wealth, the furnace of his love
in which I'll be made whole:
my sight transmuted
so I see not with my own eye
but with his; my heart transmuted
so I'm drawn, tossed lightly here and there,
loving only what he loves, seeking only
what his own heart seeks.

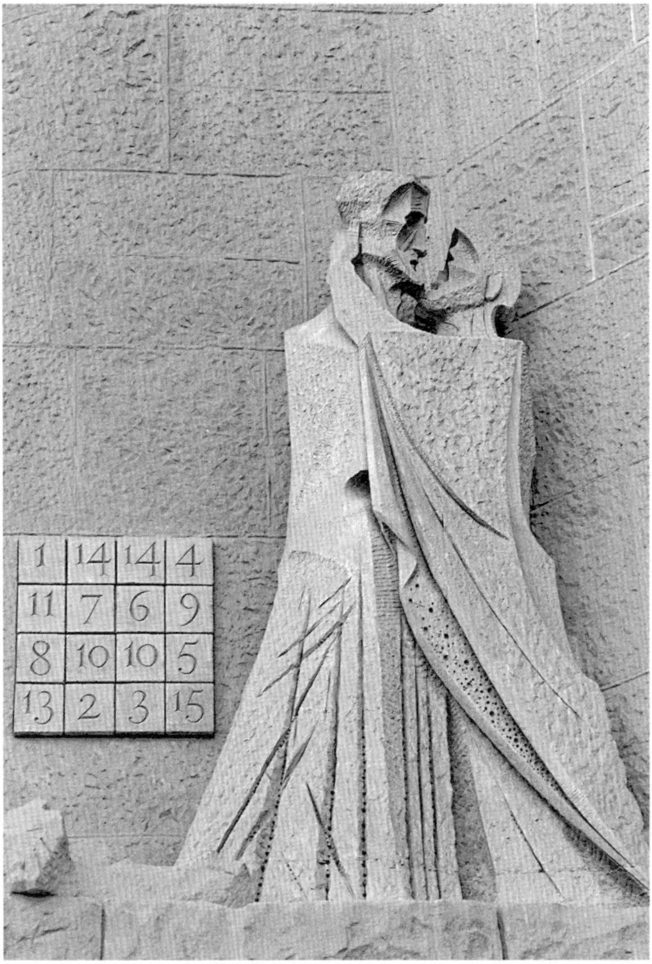
1 14 14 4
11 7 6 9
8 10 10 5
13 2 3 15

31

Se ’l breve suon, che sol quest’aer frale
circonda e move, e l’aura, che raccoglie
lo spirto dentro e poi l’apre e discioglie
soavemente in voce egra e mortale,
con tal dolcezza il cor sovente assale
che d’ogni cura vil s’erge e ritoglie,
sprona, accende il pensier, drizza le voglie
per gir volando al ciel con leggier ale,
che fia quando udirà con vivo zelo
la celeste harmonia l’anima pura,
sol con l’orecchia interna attenta al vero
dinanzi al suo fattor nel primo cielo,
u’ non si perde mai l’ampia misura
né si discorda il bel concento altero?

31

If this little music, stirring the frail air,
can gather up the spirit,
open it and melt it as it does—
If this mere breeze of sound, this mortal voice,
can lift the heart so,
heal it, startling thought and firing our resolve—
what will that heart do when,
before God in the first and ancient heaven,
it hears the music of all being?
When, struck by truth, it steps forth
in the great wind of that singing?

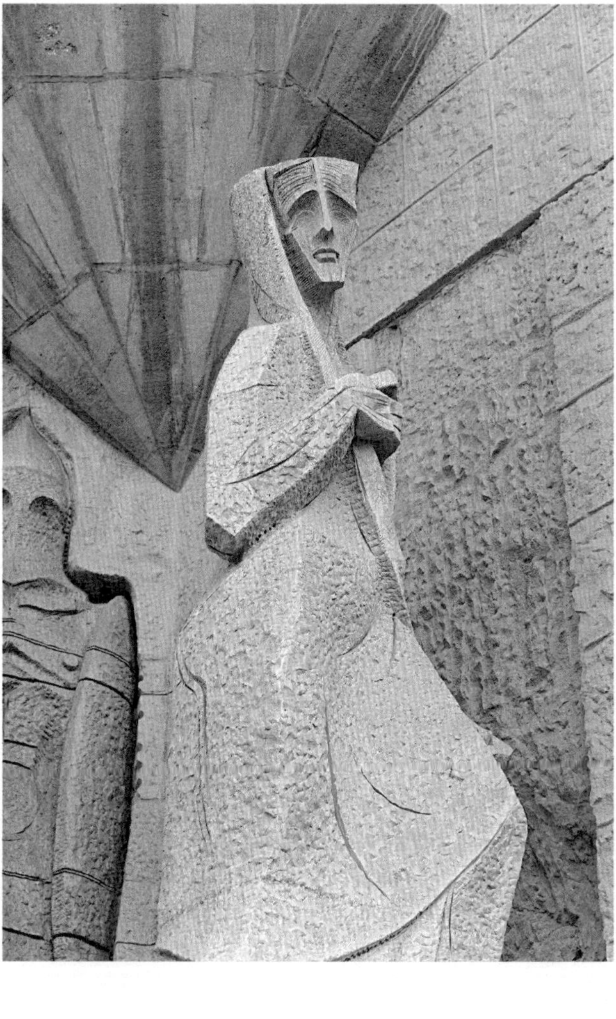

41

Quando quell'empio tradimento aperse
Iesù contra sé ordito al caro amato
discepolo, in silenzio il suo turbato
aspetto quasi a gli altri il discoperse,
ma il buon maestro il suo petto gli offerse;
e pria che fosse il duolo oltra passato
dal core e 'l viso avesse ancor bagnato,
il sonno chiuse l'occhio e il duol coverse,
ond'ei cadde in sul dolce letto, e volo
non fece augel già mai tant'alto quanto
volò in questo cader l'aquila altera.
Dio li mostrò se stesso e li fu solo
e luce e specchio, mentre ebbe quel santo
riposo in braccio a l'alta pace vera.

41

When, to the one he most loved, Jesus
opened what was in his heart,
when he spoke of the betrayal, the plot
that was to come, it broke
the heart inside his friend. In silence—
for the others must not know—
the tears cut gutters in his face.
                                        But seeing this,
his master held him to his breast,
and before the ditch of pain
had closed inside, had closed his eyes
in sleep.
            No eagle ever flew as high
as the divine one in the moment of that falling.
This was God, who was himself alone,
both light and mirror. His rest,
true rest, his sleep
true sleep, and peace.

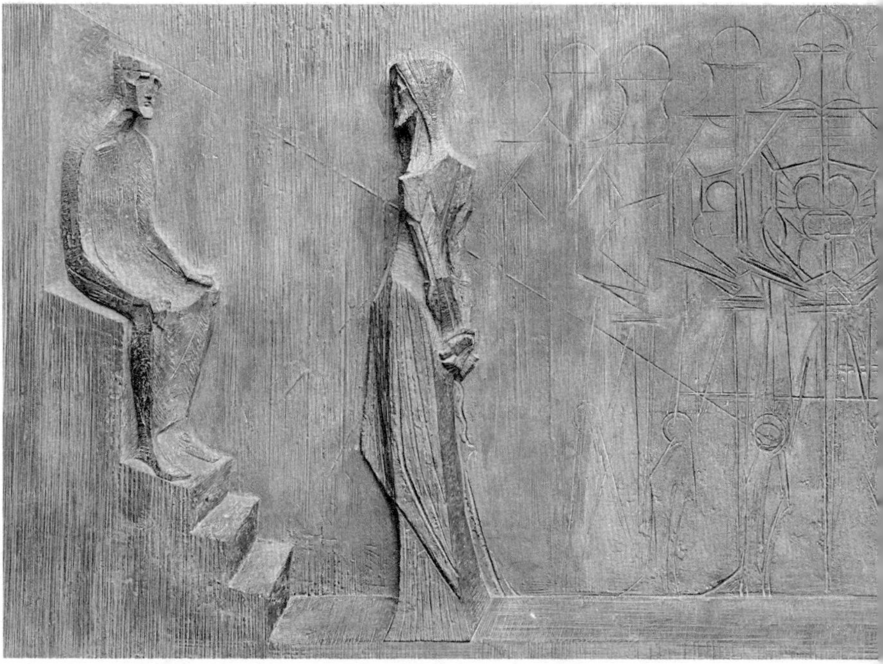

45

Mentre che quanto dentro avea concetto
dei misteri di Dio ne facea degno
la vergin Luca, oprava egli ogni ingegno
per formar vero il bel divino aspetto,
ma de l'immensa idea sì colmo il petto
avea, che come un vaso d'acqua pregno
che salir non può fuor, l'alto disegno
a poco a poco uscì manco e imperfetto.
In parte finse l'aer dolce e grave;
quel vivo no 'l mostrò, forse sdegnando
de l'arte i gravi lumi e la fiera ombra.
Basta che 'l modo umil, l'atto soave
a Dio rivolge, accende, move, e quando
si mira il cor d'ogni atra nebbia sgombra.

45

You've seen Luke's portrait of the virgin:
for all his skill, she isn't really human.
Too grave and still.
                                        At least,
that's what I used to think—
that like a vase that's overfull but has too small an opening,
what was immense within him
dribbled out, too meagre to impress.
But now I wonder if it's otherwise,
for it's certain I am moved.
Perhaps because he chose against
dramatic chiaroscuro,
he found a way to her humility.
                                                                    And it is this
that turns, inflames, and lifts my heart.
Sweeps all my doubts away.

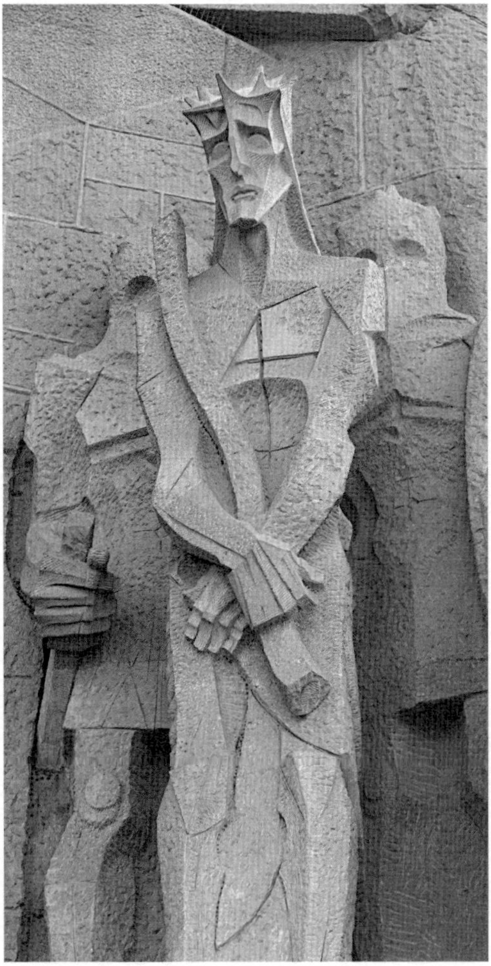

56

Questa d'odiar la morte antica usanza
nasce sovente in noi, ciechi mortali,
dal non aver su gli omer le grandi ali
ferme de la divina alta speranza,
né 'n quella pietra, ch'ogni stima avanza
di sodezza, ma solo in questi frali
fondamenti di rena a tutti i mali
exposti, edificar la nostra stanza;
onde con fede anchor per grazia spera
l'alma in Dio forte aver per segno caro
quella, ch'a i più superbi è più nemica,
e non che sia col braccio empio ed avaro
de le mie spoglie lieta, anzi io sia altera
d'usare in gloria mia la sua fatica.

56

We are blind. The ancient fear of death
assails us often, for we do not carry on our backs
the great and solid wings of hope.
Nor do we build our houses on that rock,
but dig in sand
and call our losses cruel. Yet death
is what makes room for love.
May I not hoard the mortal beauty
that surrounds me. May I learn to see instead
how, in the fire of being, suffering
is turned to light.

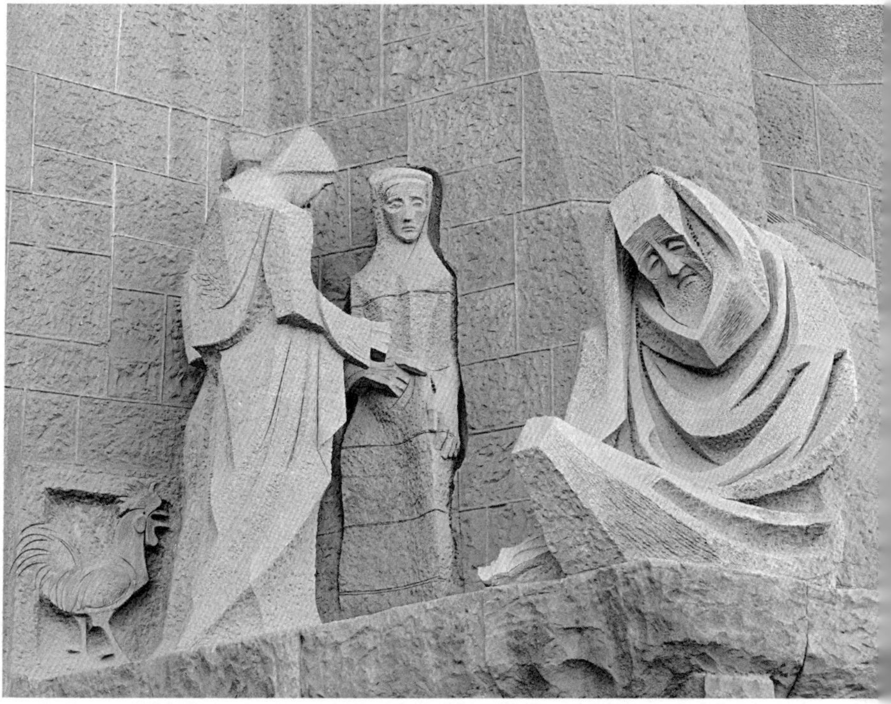

79

Non potrò dire, o mio dolce conforto,
che non sia destro il luogo, e i tempi e l'ore,
per far chiaro con l'opre un tale ardore,
quale è il desio che dentro acceso porto.
Ma se ben questo o quel picciol diporto
sottrae dal sempre procurarvi onore
i sensi, ho pur per grazia fermo il core
non mai drizzar la vela ad altro porto.
M'accorgo or che nel mondo e sterpi e spine
torcer non ponno al saggio il destro piede
dal sentier dritto s'antivede il fine;
ma il molto amore a noi, la poca fede
de l'invisibil cose alte e divine,
ne ritardano il corso a la mercede.

79

I would be lying, o sweet comfort, if I said
it's not the time or place to act upon this fervour,
the desire I bear within me, brightly lit.
But if I seem distracted, if I fail
in the attention I would always give, know this:
my heart is firm; your grace inspires it;
I will not set my sail to any other port.
You've helped me understand that pain and disappointment
cannot turn the wise man from his path.
The only thing that really slows our progress
is self-love, a weakened faith
in what is high, holy, invisible.

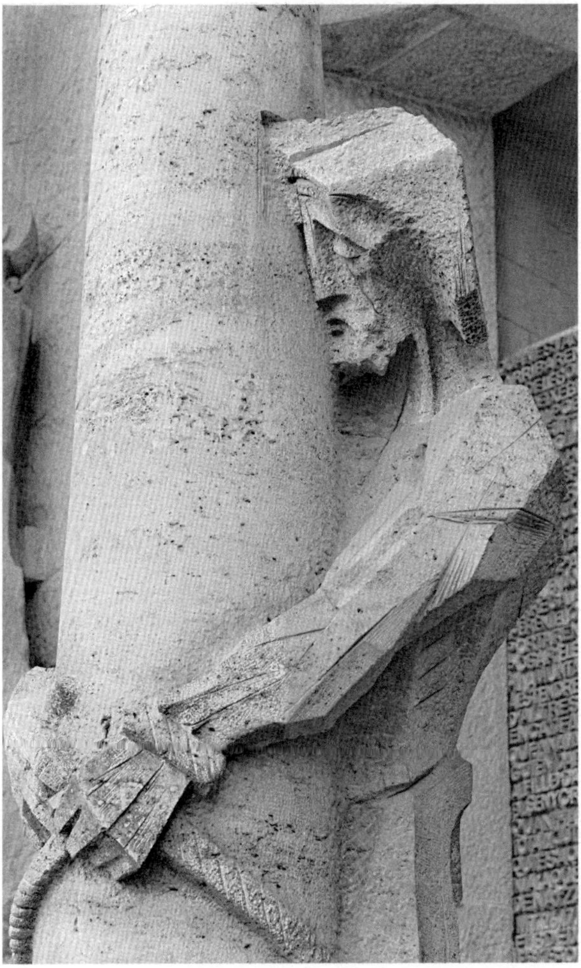

94

Qui non è il loco umil, né l'amorose
braccia de l'alta madre, né i pastori,
né del pietoso vecchio i dolci amori,
né l'angeliche voci alte e gioiose,
né dei re sapienti le pompose
offerte fatte con si vivi ardori;
ma ci sei tu, che te medesmo onori,
Signor, cagion di tutte l'altre cose.
So che quel vero che nascesti Dio
sei qui, né invidio altrui, ma ben pietate
ho sol di me non ch'io giungesi tardo,
non è il tempo infelice, ma son io
misera che per fede ancor non ardo
come essi per vederti in quella etate.

94

Here is no lowly manger, no holy mother's
happy arms; no shepherds; no sweet, old
pious man; no angel voices; no wise kings;
no gifts. Yet you
are here, my Lord, creator of all things.
As is the truth that you were born a god.
What is this longing, then?
It's not because I came too late,
nor that our age is difficult. It is.
What I envy is the faith of those first green
and shining moments. The astonished ardour
of the ones who saw.

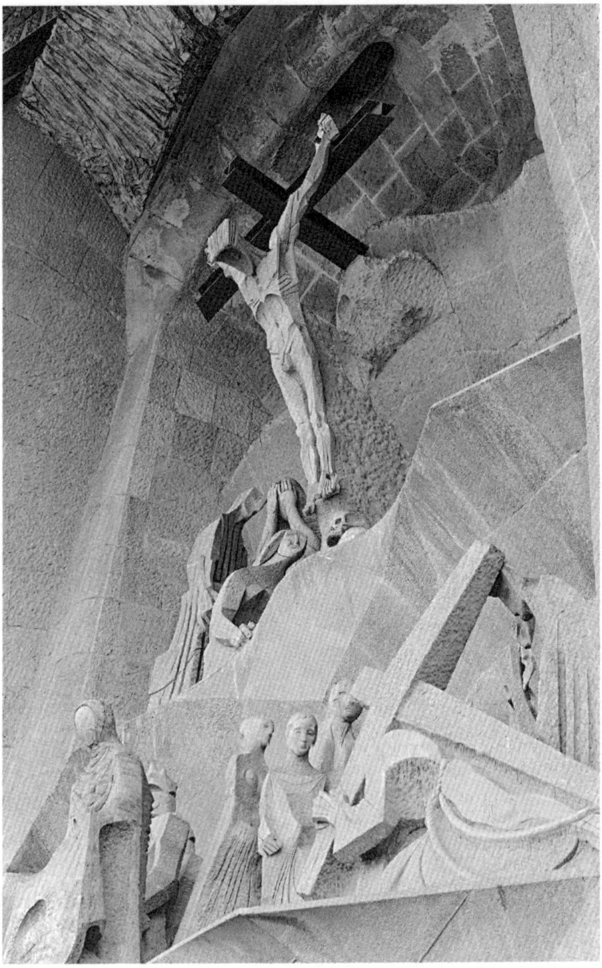

102

S'in man prender non soglio unqua la lima
del buon giudizio, e ricercando intorno
con l'occhio disdegnoso io non adorno
né tergo la mia rozza incolta rima,
nasce perché non è mia cura prima
procacciar di ciò lode o fuggir scorno,
né che dopo il mio lieto al ciel ritorno
viva ella al mondo in più onorata stima;
ma dal foco divin, che 'l mio intelletto,
sua mercé, infiamma, convien ch'escan fore
mal mio grado talor queste faville,
e s'alcuna di lor un gentil core
avien che scaldi, mille volte e mille
ringraziar debbo il mio felice errore.

102

Why, you may wonder, have I failed
to take the rasp of good sense to these
rough uncultivated verses?
But I think you know.
It isn't praise or immortality
I'm after. It's because
I do not dare. The divine fire, lovingly, in spite of me,
enflames my mind and gathers tinder
for its sparks. If a few of these, despite my clumsiness,
should sometime warm some gentle heart,
a thousand times a thousand
thanks I owe.

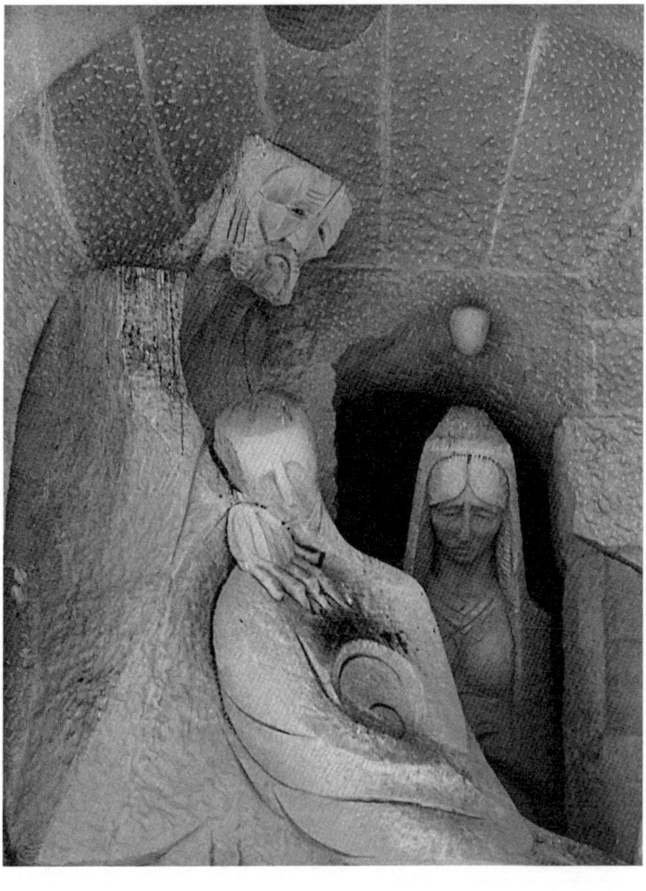

103

Temo che 'l laccio, ov'io molt'anni presi
tenni li spirti, ordisca or la mia rima
sol per usanza, e non per quella prima
cagion d'averli in Dio volti e accesi.
Temo che sian lacciuoli intorno tesi
di colui ch'opra mal con sorda lima,
e mi faccia parer da falsa stima
utili i giorni forse indarno spesi.
Di giovar poca, ma di nocer molta
ragion vi scorgo, ond'io prego 'l mio foco
ch'entro in silenzio il petto abbracci ed arda.
Interrotto dal duol, dal pianger roco
esser dee il canto vèr colui ch'ascolta
dal cielo, e al cor non a lo stil riguarda.

103

I am afraid the knot in which for years
my soul has been bound up now rules: I write
from habit, not because I am on fire.
I am afraid the knot is tightly tied,
and by myself: I'm proud
and therefore dull. I think
my days are useful
when in fact I waste them.
Come, then, flame of love:
sear me from within
again. Make me make my song
from silence and hoarse cries.
God listens only for my heart.
He cares nothing for my style.

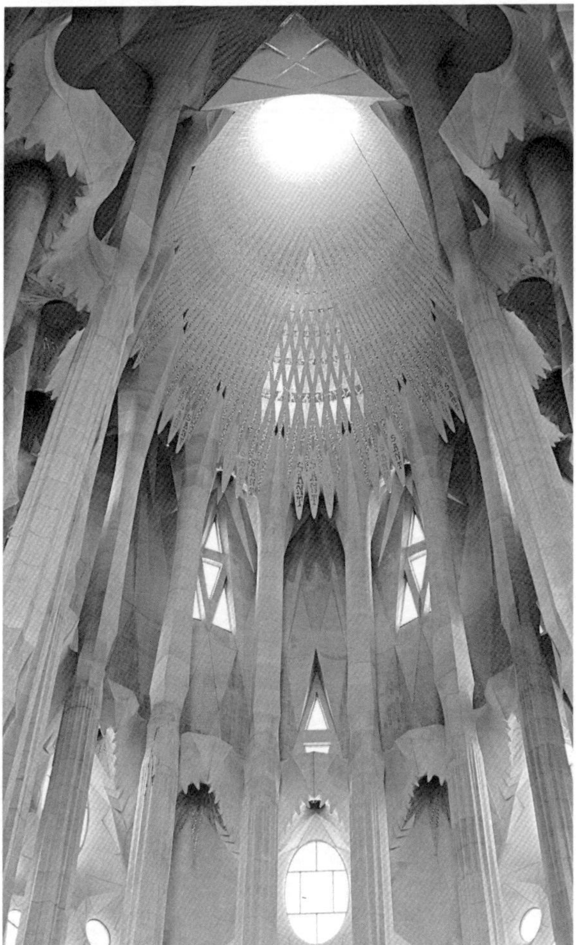

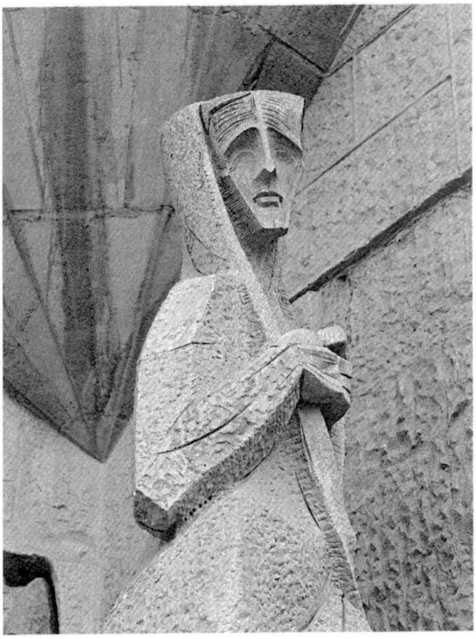

Jan Zwicky is a poet, philosopher and musician whose work is often cited for its intense lyricism. She studied philosophy at the University of Calgary, then earned her Ph.D. at the University of Toronto, and subsequently taught at a number of North American universities. She is a prolific essayist and the author of a dozen books, including *Lyric Philosophy* and *Wisdom & Metaphor*. Her poetry has won the Governor General's Award (*Songs for Relinquishing the Earth*, 1998), the Dorothy Livesay Poetry Prize (*Robinson's Crossing*, 2004), and numerous other accolades. Originally from the prairies, Zwicky now lives on Quadra Island, British Columbia.

Robert Moody is a mathematician whose professional life has revolved around the mathematics of symmetry and long-range order. Moody studied mathematics at the University of Saskatchewan and the University of Toronto, before joining the faculty at the University of Saskatchewan and, later, the University of Alberta. He is internationally recognized for his co-discovery of what are known as the Kac-Moody algebras, one of the significant advances in mathematics in the latter half of the twentieth century. His enduring pursuit of black and white photography, with its emphasis on simplicity, form and abstraction, is a visual complement to his mathematics. He is a winner of the Wigner Medal and is an Officer of the Order of Canada. He makes his residence in Victoria, British Columbia.

Bembo is an old-style humanist typeface originally cut by Francesco Griffo in 1495 and named for Pietro Bembo, a Renaissance cardinal who wrote one of the earliest Italian grammars, and later included a sonnet written in his honour by Vittoria Colonna in his own *Rime*, which he published in 1535. The typeface was revived by Stanley Morison in 1929 for the Monotype Corporation, originally with no italics. Bembo is often deemed to express classical beauty or formal tradition in typography. The version that appears on these pages has been fine-tuned by distinguished Canadian poet and typographer Robert Bringhurst, and is used with his permission.